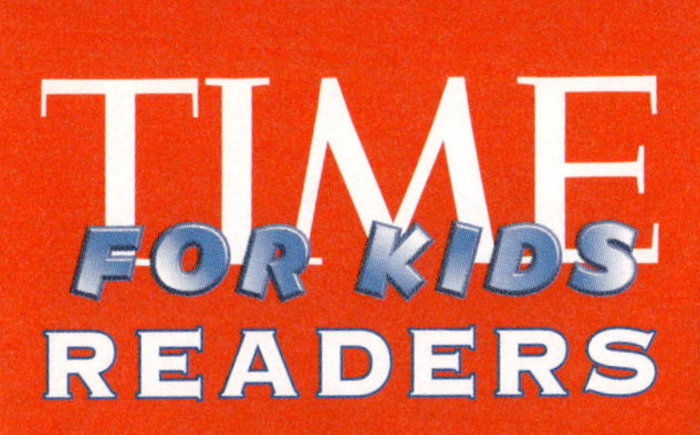

TIME FOR KIDS READERS

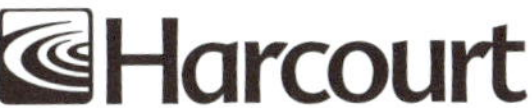

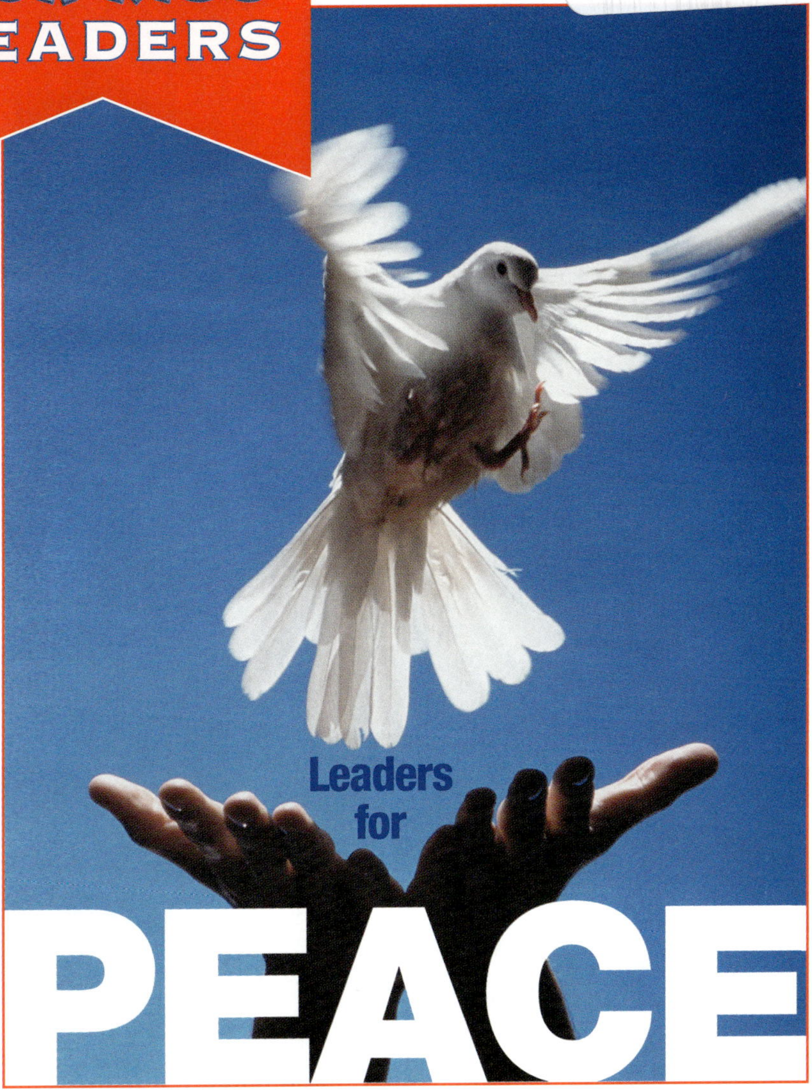

Leaders for PEACE

by Dan Ahearn

Harcourt

Orlando Austin Chicago New York Toronto London San Diego

Visit *The Learning Site!*
www.harcourtschool.com

The history of the world
is filled with people who
worked to improve lives.
In this book you will meet
a few of them: Mohandas
Gandhi, Eleanor Roosevelt,
Mother Teresa, and
Archbishop Desmond Tutu.

MOHANDAS K. GANDHI
1869-1948

Mohandas Gandhi was born in 1869 in Porbandar, India. At that time, India was ruled by Britain. The people of India were not treated fairly. Gandhi believed changes should be made.

After studying law in England, Gandhi worked in South Africa. When he returned to India, he did not like the way that the British government ruled the country. He wanted India to rule itself.

Gandhi believed that violence must never be used. People who believed as Gandhi did quit their British government jobs and refused to buy goods made by the British. Gandhi led the Indian people in peaceful protest marches against the British government.

In 1947, the British government agreed they would no longer rule India. Gandhi proved that change can happen without using violence. Millions of people respected and admired Gandhi. They called him the "Mahatma," which means "great souled."

Eleanor Roosevelt
overcame her shyness
to give speeches. She
also went on trains to
campaign with her
husband.

Before Eleanor Roosevelt, the wives of politicians were not very involved in American politics. When her husband, Franklin D. Roosevelt, became ill, Eleanor began to work for the Democratic Party. She soon saw that this was a way that she could help people improve their lives.

After Franklin D. Roosevelt got better, he could no longer walk. Eleanor helped him run for public office again. He became President of the United States in 1933. President Roosevelt couldn't travel well. He asked Eleanor to travel with him and help him with his work. She went where the President could not.

During a coal miner's strike, Eleanor Roosevelt went to the mines. She saw what the problems were. She saw how bad it was in the mines. When she returned to Washington, she tried to improve the miners' lives. When World War II came, she visited American soldiers around the world.

After her husband's death, Eleanor didn't stop working. She spoke out for equal rights. She wrote books. She represented the United States in the United Nations. Today, Eleanor Roosevelt is remembered as a great woman.

MOTHER TERESA 1910-1997

Mother Teresa's real name was Agnes. Her parents were Albanians living in Macedonia. When Agnes was 18, she entered the religious order of the Sisters of Our Lady of Loretto. She took the name of Saint Teresa, the special saint of missionaries. Missionaries spend their lives spreading religious teaching to other countries.

She was sent to India as a teacher. She worked in Calcutta, a city with some of the poorest people in India. Some of the people had no homes and were sick. They didn't have money for a hospital. Mother Teresa was disturbed by their suffering.

Mother Teresa receives the Nobel Peace Prize.

In 1950, Mother Teresa started her own religious order, The Missionaries of Charity. They spend their lives helping the poor. In 1952, Mother Teresa opened a home in Calcutta for the sick. There, the sick were cared for and given a peaceful place to live.

In 1979, Mother Teresa was awarded the Nobel Peace Prize. This prize is given every year to the person who has done the most for the cause of peace.

ARCHBISHOP DESMOND TUTU 1931-

Desmond Tutu was born in South Africa. At that time, there were laws in South Africa that forced people who were not white to live apart from others. He worked to change those unfair laws.

Tutu became a priest in 1960. He was the first black man to have this job in his church. Later, he was the first black Archbishop of Capetown.

Tutu believed he could change the unfair laws of South Africa without violence. He spoke out and he led marches for equality. In 1984, he was awarded the Nobel Peace Prize for his work.

Archbishop Tutu speaks to his congregation in Capetown, South Africa.

Desmond Tutu reached his goal when Nelson Mandela was chosen as the first black president of South Africa. It was the first election in which all the people of South Africa were able to vote. Desmond Tutu is a true leader of peace.

Nelson Mandela, the first black leader of South Africa, has worked with Archbishop Tutu.